If You Keep Making that

S **H** A M E **F** A **C** E...

If You Keep Making that SHAMEFACE...

POEMS

CJ Farnsworth

Sheila-Na-Gig Editions

ACKNOWLEDGMENTS

Some poems in this collection were previously published, often in earlier versions, as cited:

Appalachian Review: "Desire"
Backbone Mountain Review: "Paint Strip"
Bluestone Review: "Fresh Cut Grass Smell"
Community College Humanities Review Journal: "Playing the Ingénue"
Impost: "Bliss"
Kestrel: "Advice for the naked baby I found in the snow"
Rattle: "Swim"
Women Speak, Vol. 5: "Drawing in Four-Color Ballpoint Pen"
Women Speak Vol. 6: "some rare but serious side effects may include"
Women Speak Vol. 7: "Severstal Re-Opens the Yorkville Plant in Time for Christmas"
Women Speak Vol. 8: "Uvalde"

For every girl who's ever felt she's not enough

or been told she's a little too much.

Only the self need watch the self
and only the self need shame the self.

—*The Psychology of Shame*, Dr. Gershen Kaufman

CONTENTS

I

II

III

IV

I

SHAME TURNS ATTENTION TO THE FACE...
BLUSHING, FOR EXAMPLE, ONLY COMPOUNDS
SHAME, CAUSING ONE EVEN TO FEEL ASHAMED OF SHAME.

—KAUFMAN

Drawing in four-color ballpoint pen

If I love mom I have to love dad
and if I love dad I have to love fat, blind
brother and if I love fat, blind brother I have to love cottage cheese
grandma and if I love cottage cheese
grandma I have to love cigarette pap and if I love cigarette
pap I have to love gold lame' granny and if I love gold lame'
granny I have to love the Kojak guy she's married to
now and if I love that Kojak guy I have to love
the pee dog and if I love the pee dog I have to love
Aunt Penny with a crew cut and no teeth
who throws chairs and if I love hairless, toothless, chair-throwing
Penny I have to love dirty pennies in parking
lots and if I have to love grubby pennies in parking
lots I have to love the spidery
space beneath the basement steps
and if I love the spider space
beneath the basement steps I have to love
the dark, the web, the flies and everything
that's caught and stuck
and preyed upon and praying

The Day Some Lady Said It's Too Late Now

Frank O'Hara died 56 years ago now
Not sure how and I'm not going to Google it, not now
He was about a decade younger than I am now
It's 1:36 p.m. and I have 16¢ in my bank account, pending now
One son who is preparing to leave home now
A wall covered by degrees and I am a CSR now
Meaning I serve customers who prefer to be served now
If I, or they, knew what Gauloises are, I might get them a carton
    if they wanted one now
Though it seems like Gauloises are cigarettes and those aren't
    as sought after now
In this green cathedral, well, tobacconists
    would be fuckfaces now
The only Frank here is a Midland Painted Turtle, at least right now
Sinatra, the snake, is in the infirmary over at the zoo
    with some kind of mouth rot now
The latest boss quit Friday, so everyone's gathering in her office
    to giggle now
I'm sunk in a trench of succulents that only need water
    every 2-3 weeks now
The public Wifi password is 1234567890, c'mon now
Mail to kids at Camp Giscowheco can be sent to 237 Juliette Way
    but love is viral now
3 weeks ago a waif I knew a while ago blew up her liver
    1,246 likes circulate now
My face is no social place for all the Dear Johns, john doors,
    Porta Johns, trending now
I have 3 chicken tenders and raw carrots for lunch
    and I'm getting hungry now
The lady who died was Billie Holiday, I know that now
Hurt finds a place to hide, I can hear it now
As kids carve pumpkins, glaze moons, try to capture life, slide
    a shoebox onto the desk, repeat the same question:
What now?
What should I do now?

Can you take it now?
As a kid presses his back against the wingspan wall
    saying, "Which am I now?"
Sharp-shinned hawk 17-24 in
American crow 2.8-3.3 ft
Red-tailed hawk 3.5-4.5 ft
Great-horned owl 4-5 ft
Bald eagle 6-7.5 ft
I lift the lid, take one look at a hatchling nestled in an old sock
    and say, "It's too late now"
The man says to the boy, "You are an American crow, for now"
The man opens the door and the boy asks about the box now
"Some lady said it's too late now"
I write 10 a.m. - 5 p.m. / 7 hours
    on my timesheet before I forget
I am some lady now

Miss Average

My head fell off this morning—a nose hit.
Why do we try to get it all right? Get a strike?

Feeling, finally, my split, I'm inspired to dump
the ball, to reckon with its stutter through the gutter.

Tulips: clean sheets
Daffodils: debutante pins
Peonies: the guillotine

I lofted my body at *Les Misérables*, *A Tale of Two Cities*,
Floriography and often thought critically of lobbing heads.

Sliding down blocked lanes—all night open bowling—that awful
frame of development. I write to you because I see your pillory,
see you lugging around your severed head, flashing your fake ID.

There is the sizing and sheathing of feet, the creeping around
gripping holes to test your strength
to be sure you can toss your weight.

The guillotine was merciful, comparatively, it was said.
Ideas are no good no more because we're condemned
to see their heads.

Who isn't skeptical of virtue?
We've had Uncles enough.

Pillaged/pillager roiling on the hotdog roller,
all the onions sucked dry.

Squeeze your grip sack. Your grandmothers did.
But who can I speak for? My girl face is stuck in the return.

Bowling alleys are hard to find
these days—all holy sites.

Blood Drive

I fill a bag with my blood and give it away. I've been feeling purposeless and they're having a Superbowl tickets giveaway. When I ask the woman taking my blood about blood, she tells me she drove across the country for a vacation[1] and never went back and asks if I know what it feels like when an elephant is off your shoulders. She says two of her children stayed back, they're old enough anyway. She says her son never liked school, no way, but his name's on a satellite now anyway. While I watch the red river of me flow, I try to picture the bridge connecting her to her son and her son to his satellite and his satellite to all the people on earth who know what it feels like when an elephant is off your shoulders, to all the elephants in Africa, and to another type native to India as well, and the elephants to their babies because it's my understanding that elephants are the best mourners in the animal kingdom and not just because it looks like they're crying all the time when really they lack the stuff to shed a tear, and elephants to the circus, specifically the acrobats and the nets below them when they're learning how to walk across a high wire, to illaqueation, to the trapped fish, turtles, maybe even baby whales because those blubbery beasts are magnificent mourners as well, to how I've heard the more they try to get out the worse it gets, to the Lotus Eaters, to ichor and faulty gods, to salty fries and how long it takes to walk them off, to journeying and how we all need to share and share and share that, how we move and grow and lose and know, to a leukocyte god and father, to the old bearded guy, shoulders bent over a Mac Book, at the check-in table who couldn't see my driver's license and didn't offer me a T-shirt or bumper sticker even though I was one of the first in line. I don't think I am ever really where I am and I can't find a bridge to get there. The woman says I have given as much blood as I can and I tell her I know. I do know what it feels like when an elephant is off your shoulders, she tells me I saved a life, then I cut through the blood line, long now, to leave.

---

[1] To the red, blue town where I'm blood bound in chokehold yore a suspended bridge circus elephants swayed parade and boom boom Buster Browns stand still moving is dicey—here she was saved

Bliss

It's on us
>because we follow it
>into all manner
>of weather
>botox-embracing
>its deep, deep kiss
>hypnotic teeth, thaumaturgic
>tongue, though
it's hard to blame us
>for huddling on foggy docks
>come monsoons
>noir-wailing on buckled
>bird legs for want
>of our knotweed
>our heart-shaped leaves
>our tiny white flowers
>dropped blooming.
Look at us, fashion plates
>Jenny Lind fan
>in one hand, snapped
>stiletto in the other
>silk embroidery
>snagged, mascara
>down our throats
>standing in our own
>hoary deadheads
gasping
I am nothing without you.

keyhole

through a mother
you espy   the world
through   fitting room   mirrors
you spy on women and stamp them
with apostrophes   you cut blanks
contraction   omission   duplication
when the smiths   study you
you carve   out your waist
unfurl your tape   /   less woman
hollowed out   a pullout couch
lean season   looming   incessant
squirrels, skunks   bears prepare
mother   less   woman
can't   catch it
identity
stare   locked
inside   reflection
blank   profile
love well
you've
peeked
you have
peaked

Rant Against Roses

So what Roses Red, I've had a drink or two so I'm just going to say it: All you got is pretty. Way to make a girl's head droop. Why not hand me a rabid raccoon? Cowboy boots? Like we're in a saloon? God's sake, you've never been horseback. Romeo, puh-leez. Why not peacock with a python piggyback, blare 80s synth from your shoulder pads, drop invites to your waterbed? It's sad, your white picket bedjacket. Chocolate-choked oaths and altar wine—oh so memetic. Pretty. That's all. You flushed cheese puff. Everyone's all "Bud" 'til the sun comes up and someone asks "Why?" Oh how prickly you get, how quickly you pull pistols, 'til you're sickly, prone, alone, dehydrated in your frou-frou bib and tucker in a truck stop pot. Your love lecture, ahem, to sum: a rosé, a tub 'n' rub, a velvet fella, a smallish green-screen biopic, especially for the empty, unfulfilled, ugly, average, odd, but that's the trouble with Elvis, stamens, and square jaw stipulations—see Pal, everyone feels duped. When you fall, get up, now, and hide your bruises—we hear you, Red. Hey Red, I wonder if you heard what Daisy said: Take a minute, Mama, lay low 'til your moonless eyes aren't so swoll. Hey, Red, you seen Poppy lately? She's three nights/week @ Con Alma, close your eyes, you'd swear Etta was there. Look Norma, you're nothing but fade, the art of shade. It's all you got. Pretty. You're a scarlet letter, Hester. I am so on to you Wonder Bread, Twinkies, Spam, spam folder fodder, OG IG filter face— pretty. And that's all. Best bush on the block? Ha! You tell everyone you're centerfold. I heard even kitsch ditched you when you showed up at her mom's funeral blotto, in a limo, with lotto tickets to raffle. All your psychobabble about lovey-doves, the gardener in a glasshouse, the queen in her card castle. Just. Pretty. Ugh! A rose is a rose is a dead horse head, a sex death knell, a bloodless missionary algorithm, a you've-really-let-yourself-go grave, maybe lose a few pounds or put 'em on Poundcake, pinky-ring Ay-Papi loves a plump peduncle. Give. Me. A. Break. Rosy. Just wait 'til your straight, sunken hips break after your first slip. All. You. Got. Is. Pretty. And take off those damn frames. I imagine throwing you in a tar pit like an adoring fan at the feet of Maria Callas. If only you were a piquant radish bouquet or a fruity head with some circuity. I think tar pits exist. Granny moved to Tarpon Springs and laid you down in the kitchen. She was a terrible cook. Thorny bitch, you've anchored yourself to all the wrong tropes. I'm sick of hedging, every rented tux knows you've pricked the wrong side of history. You know what, it's you and corn, petal-to-kernel, stem-to-stalk. In the spirit of self-awareness, you smell bad. Methinks you doth too much blush. I mean, grapevine clocks you kvetching non-stop … honestly, classic victim mentality: you didn't get to pick a path, you believed what they wanted you to believe, you can't climb getting clipped. You know what you potboiler bombshell, I should thank you dozens of times over—you're teaching me a little something about cultivation, about the necessity of agency.

Flu Z Son

Mayzie, I think about you often
in certain sicko hazes, on a red eye to Vegas
with a bald eagle, at a farmer's market in Fresno
with some pawing old hawk.
Or alone, south of the border
bartending in some beach shack
long for a sea cure. There has to be an excuse
for you. This has to be bird flu.
See, I gutted the pillows. Thereby
creating conditions to attend to.
Someone must tend, be tender.
Who doesn't love Horton—his Hippocratic
trunk—his feet like the white tails
of deer—his eyes like the underside
of a turtle's neck. To be sick is to be under
attack. My stomach caught in the aftermath
of a live-plucking. The aftermath
is always most sickening. I'm fevered
and presently fever vocabulary is grossly
rudimentary. Maybe, Mayzie, vocabulary
is too clumsy for you, not Horton, who is
himself, a little clunky. Horton portends, Mayzie
while you are a pretender. While you plan
a masquerade, a black and white ball
in the manner of Truman Capote's before
his own illness descended. Perhaps someone
like Marianne Moore, known for linguistic
precision, will show up with words
for a cure or step-by-step instructions for
whimsical mask making. I'm fond of the word
perhaps. Perhaps perhaps is a compulsion.
Once examined, there's no separating
the malady, the cause, the care. I noticed
your bags packed, but I have gathered
feathers. Let me know how the party goes

—how you see yourself. I'll be sweating it out
in this swan bevy. I hear Horton cracking eggs.
Soon his trunk will be pressed to the fever.

Advice Gleaned From a Chance Encounter With Someone I Barely Knew During the Reagan Administration

Keep what you want and let the rest wash away.
That's a bunch of hogwash, my gram would say
nothing washes away.

And it's true. I've tried bleach and blades but every blink
every wink creeps up like honeysuckle
on the cerebral chain-link.

Overgrown, teeming with bees, it blots out the fence.
Remember that song about a fly climbing a tree as high
as high could be only to fall and shatter?

I fell in love with that. I thought she wanted to understand
wingless life a little better and maybe got too tired
too high with no end in sight

in any one of her thousand eyes which brought everything
into focus. To take in the landscape and not get
the picture—it's shattering.

Let's not forget she's a pest looking toward rapture
the kind reserved for spruce, redwood, and ash
not to mention birds.

I couldn't stop thinking about flies forever, carnal garbage
grunts, shit-squatters—it sounds sickening
but it isn't, it's just a shattered fly.

Its compound eyes breaking light in a thousand different
directions. Yes, I remember being *It*. What if
you were *It* forever?

Catching broken light and piecing it together, one step
after another. Maybe she was looking to change
the sky. Do you remember this picture?

On the left edge, top bleacher, squinting, in linen
with cherries stitched on the lapel, that's me.
Do you remember Nancy Reagan's

eggs and the ozone ripped open? They say the ozone
is finally healing, opening its blue kimono
to show off its scar which is just

a thin, flat line. Like an autoharp string. Do you remember
the autoharp? An autoharp uses buttons
to play chords. It's a zither

and we shouldn't forget that or the way a fly shatters.
You kept my scratch-n-sniff Valentine in your Levi's
all this time? I can almost make out your face.

Sink or

Mother fast-friended Daddy's distant pool cousins
so to be sure we could swim
in their kidney with a corkscrew
we bit our tongues as mother jerked
orange floaties up to our throats
and yanked our hair under latex blossoms
while we kicked and screamed and held
our breath with arms over our ears
as they roared *kick/jump/keep your mouth shut*
while Daddy's-Mama's-Brother's-Girl
smoked menthols on a chaise
in a gold bandeau drinking
gin after gin after gin
because, Mother said, once upon a time
she was a beauty queen before
she had a boy with sugar they called 'Tink'
and Katrina with gold skin
and gold hair
and gold ankle
bracelets who sometimes showed
up with a long-haired/shirtless/round-shouldered
boy to pick-up a few bucks
while I snuck into the house
to use the pink drunk
bathroom that was inside
Daddy's-Mama's-Brother's-Girl's bedroom
to sit at her wicker beauty desk
wondering why the sun
made my skin red not gold
to clip on earrings that hung
like grape bunches
before sloshing out sliding doors
to the slab patio
beside the pool
convinced Bo Derek's

bedroom must be just like this
until Mother announced it was getting late
until we packed into our green Pontiac
until Mother, as heavy as the wet towels
she piled in my arms
told me to put 'em up
until I pinned each towel
until all the corners touched

Hey Momma,

Anyways, so many spiders, all year.
I leave them to their work. Like you did,
I envy their legs with loud eyes.
It seems like you holding on to snow
long April like the beech tree just won't
let go and I'm surprised, Momma, because
you were not one for ghosts. Most of ours
spent their haunts alive, you said.
On both sides, ours were glad to say
goodbye, dead, so I know the thick
apple skin isn't you, just that it's tough
and hard to chew. That's probably
just my West Coast open-ocean thinking
I still do, what you called fancy flights
so devoted to your common sense
cult. Now that you've been dead
so long, I see through your care.
Snooping, I found your sketchbook
and kept it. All those smudged apples
and ears. In back, a few nudes.
Charcoal fingerprints. You always said
spiders mind their business, to make
my business my own. Probably why
I still call on Sundays and keep
my flies windpiped. At night, though
when squirrels wake the arcade
I skitter up to the attic and stick
my sticky fingers out to see how many
tickets I can snag—it sure does
seem like you, though, keeping score.

Meaning "Dear One"

So much talk of happiness seems sad.
I want an emotion of my own and a tulip
bud plucked from its stem
because it reminds me of my son's head
when he was born, the pistachio-shaped bulb
purple and ready to burst is what
I remember of birth—and the part
I was playing, Cherie, when at three months
his soft spot ballooned and his spine
was tapped as I took the stage
wearing a pink gardenia and a black teddy
then hustled out the backstage door
so I could sleep beside his crib
in the PICU humming *That Old Black Magic*
as the IV, keeping his tender
(and there is no better word—tender)
bran new body alive, dripped potion
into his cheeselike arm. Bran, just
separated from the husk, not yet
ready for the 'd,' still a soft-bodied kyrie—
like elemenopee, not yet able to stand
or hold up his head as I hummed
down 'n' down, round 'n' round I go
running my tongue along my teeth.
Teeth are present at birth, present
when the baby's head first presents
at the mouth of the uterus, just waiting
behind the proscenium curtain
for the cue to burst into the spotlight
for a standing ovation.

Shortcake

Lying under a thin sheet, I might be praying for my son's brain.
Who knows if nakedness and repetition, if urgently and emphatically
seeking fixes adequately constitutes prayer.
God is not Aladdin. God is not Walt Disney.
Here it is: I have a beautiful boy, a bona fide bloodpump.
Here I am— a harpsichord.
I've taken a hammer to counterpoint. Evidence is mounting
I'm preoccupied with preludes.
I'm legless, keyless, highly ornamental, a misshapen pearl.
You know, Baroque.
Now my son does not feel centered. My plectrum *is* plastic.
He's plucked, in the sense of birthlessness.
Here I am, strings aquiver. Like Pastor's wife
Ms. Patsy said: let the children be little like a light of mine
in the north night shines. Go ahead, cut out the candle.
Largely, it's about submission. No doubt part of the problem.
And fix.
So I'm fumbling through a wood box, a treasure chest my son
gave me when I seemed big, full of rocks he'd painted
each with a red heart but they've been lost forever.
Where does it go?
Does it fall heavy, hot-mouthed like this dog?
Does it melt like a fat flake of snow under the moon's scrutiny?
In the kitchen, rotting bananas smell like prayers ready
to be bread. Bread, talk about centricity! Prayers
probably hit similar themes, easily grouped.
Maybe I should be manifesting? Arresting my vagrant ego?.

Either way, here goes:
Please displace the anguine shadow of me, the sour beet of me
from my son's holyish pearl. Let's make it concrete, so
maybe in time for his birthday late spring, just as strawberries begin
to peak just before the Grace Evangelical Lutheran Church celebrates

strawberries, mostly in the parking lot
where they put up a money wheel where
one dollar might mean two or twenty or none.
I remember in the days before bingo, most people
didn't even go inside for shortcake.

My son texts: where r u????

sitting in the parking lot outside the gym
because it just keeps getting harder the going
in thinking about how you are not dead
because you are not dead i cant get to the
bottom of my compulsion for this kind of
calisthenics but ive always favored using my
body against itself i say fat first i deadlift
your life youre my treadmill gut crunch
resistance band ankle weight tracking the
impacts of your jacked up nocturnality is my
artspace on planet fitness tricep press is the
most popular machine its easy to bear down
on an immense stack cheat strength eat fries
please cut back ive stopped obsessing over
the Mütter Museum i feed birds now the
squirrels pillage them worse the chickadees
wrens even the punk jays dont seem to know
or care i cant tell if they do anything but
survive whens it enough ive started growing
basil parsley mint i went looking for ramps
your dad says its a shame his pal got worked
out by the heavyweights who bought his
family biz for dimes and i say say addict one
more time about your uncle buried under
Jims beam keep adding plates oh and ... i left
our inside tree out the t-rex tree i knew
the days were losing weight i knew the
weeks were growing weak i knew the T
lacked endurance not sturdy i knew it didn't
stand a chance yet i watched it frost wheeze
plead i killed it im figuring out how to live
with that you probably havent seen the
corpse by the door on purpose so im forced
to face my ruin as Xmas approaches every

time the dog pees and anytime you come to
crash laughing or trying not to laugh im
always nearby sometimes i catch the moon
smirking like it knows the truth about
working things out   —your mother

pitstop

buy your vape vials
cigarettes, CBD, beer
and scratch-offs
do not mind
my boy who
you will not recognize
as mine
curls, skin, Hey Dudes
the color of boiled peanuts
if you see him
in Speedway or Circle-K
along whatever highway
you're taking to escape
it's his birthday (almost)
I can't stop it
and it doesn't stop
without me
so I douse him in
cautionary tales of men (almost)
& the history of heartbreak
just like I did with
sunblock and bug spray
so stranger
from the pit of me
I ask you to
take off your strange face
and put your kind on
if you happen by
my boy (you won't recognize as mine)
stopped to pee
or for sweet tea
like the kind
of kindness
of strangers
who leave clean water
outside
for strays
slinking by

Feather Boa

One of the hardest things to do in this life is
to be yourself. It is easy to be other people and
things. We are born performers, though most of us
never make it big.

My favorite part is still bird.
Some days a crow heavy and dark, mystery and slick.
Some days a bully blue jay
when there's not enough of me inside me
to face the shape of my face, my nosewings.

Being all you are is what makes it hard.
I mean, how we came is it
so it's change, change, change
migratory patterns, talons, teeth.

Some days a finch, a painted bunting.
When you see her you think it's your birthday
and everyone's brought a gift
that's a metaphor for who you are.

Some days a chickadee—so pleased with her hidden
nests and seeds, with all the me's she hides
in tree hollows, blowholes, sand burrows.

Best is her song, chickadee-dee-dee-dee-dee-dee
that makes you feel safe enough to rest your forehead
in her neck frock.

Off bird days, I have a well-developed rodeo clown
more hula-hoop pants, square-dance
and Oh, the red-nose though!

The world sees a you you'll never see. Wild.
You see the world as … should you moonwalk
you will never see the world.

Best advice I've ever received: Next time you feel cold
and exposed, ogle the boundary between earth 'n' sky,
be sure there are trees, you'll notice how they leave
fingerprints on the dividing line.

It used to be no one believed in life
on other planets, but now
no one can reasonably believe we are alone.

II

Or the self may hang its head inside
while outwardly displaying defiance.

—Kaufman

Wordsworth, What Now?

Nonetheless commando, bust down the door, head purring
heart moaning, and let them know you play for keeps.

Send your heart out to sea. Let it bloom with jellyfish, bulk
up with walrus, but do not let shame sharpen your tusks.

Do not keep it to yourself. Do not get caught in that net.
Let puffins nest where arrows pierce your most innerness.

In due time they will fledge, free of your blubber and stew.
Let every arrow be pyric, beget lyrics. Let yourself discover

the elementals and leave your fingerprints, your underwear
at the banquet in bouquets, too. Nonetheless, this circle

is etched, so you must thumb up, you must set and shoot
the surging remembering is here for you too, to create your

self anew and anew and anew

no matter what the cat eyes make of you. Nonetheless, Words
worth, I address my wistful wish to you, that Bill in Boston

picks his Dreadnought every Wed. for everyone in the world
howling all hours. Great God! My bosom bared, just his long

fingers on its neck as he rises from the sea of us I hear him
plucking *Smoke on the Water* lifetimes ago in his mom's

garage, chords up-gathering in her Plymouth, heart up-gathering
in his throat, stars up-gathering in his eyes a nascent shine.

Nonetheless, alone in front of my phone listening to Bill jam
alone, in front of his phone, I cannot imagine anything too much.

Newsfeed Circum Planet Fitness

Princess Diana and the Titanic are back, but I love the psychedelic
weather map.

If you were a tragedy, what kind of tragedy would you be?
And why? Victim of a shark attack.

Standing, maybe up to the thigh, hands on hips, thong,
knee popped.

All the beach people would say they didn't see it coming.
She wasn't out too deep. Followed by, did you know
sharks have nictitating eyes?

Meaning their eyeballs roll back when they eat.
It's like they see with their teeth. Senses overlap, it's true.
You can taste what you smell before you open your mouth.

I mean, any sense at all they'd have felt the freak fish darting
before the tuba started throbbing, before
I got cinched.

They would have heard the way I tasted on that shark's papillae.
They'd have smelled all the no's before I was halved.

Maybe one woman, probably my mother, does hear the hunger coming
so she stands up. Yes, hand shading her eyes, she walks toward me
pointing and snaking her finger like people do
when they mean for you to come.

And I would. I would walk just in time, sun-blind, on my two whole legs
back to my towel, to friends eating foot long hot dogs
they didn't pay for, ketchup plopping into their belly holes.

Death Valley is solid red, pressing the record, and Lake Mead
is evaginating.

What if Earth was on *The Dating Game?*

Earth would have taken Hurricane Hannah or Wildfire Wilbert.
She'd want us to feel it before we could see it, before
we could hear it or smell it or taste

—she's nobody's tragedy.

Soup for Brains

it's a stone crock
of vichyssoise out there

potatoes are the only lovable
poverty trait

I grow best buried
and have lots of eyes

I can't remember anything in
winter but r

lowercase, as in li'l ms running
rutabaga

rudimentary or just rude
reckless, relentless, synonyms

for vicious, I've always imagined
synonyms swinging, lining up

upside-down pineapples, pink lawn
flamingos for Saturnalia season

reckless takes off her -less to hop
in the pot ride-that-train style

sex is like soup in the snow
or, sun-speaking, like citrus

for old-time sailors who told
themselves there were new worlds

to grab and hold, new worlds
that were already old

discovery unravels the quilt
and steals the needle

lays in the human heart
something like dynamite

and if the vowels go missing
sbjgtn nd dsplcmnt, so what

it's the quest for x, to mark
a spot before the pot boils over

before the whistle blows on sus x
the pissy epistemology too long

burning burnt down the house
I was home when it caught fire

took full of smoke so when
my mother buried the wishbone

for someone to get rando lucky
I snuck in and stole it

to break the bone alone
to win at wishing

Madrigal, Because I Say So

O, the open window, sometimes I wonder
how we breathe at all.

Lawnmowers puff up a savory soufflé.
Summer hangs like a full silk slip on the line.

I know slips are over, but I need to believe
in once softer, simpler times.

Full of fresh cravings and guilt over starving,
I listen as a boy hands Summer over

to his mother, "Keep it, but keep your eyes
open." Another woman, like most

of the world I expect, seems to be making
plans to celebrate someone moving on

with life. Her hands blossom on the asphalt.
I loath fingernails, it's odd & nothing

to be proud of, but filing is one way
to measure growth. Moving is one way

to give up. Sometimes giving up is another
way to measure growth. A good many

don't give up on life with their dying breath
though they come to accept a jaggy nail.

Do as Summer does. Walk through
the temple of tomatoes, the blue haven

of berries, the sacristy of zucchini.
Observe Summer's give so you can learn

to live with its take. Just this Summer
I learned that Mary anointed Jesus' feet

with nard and he said we'll always have
the poor. Turns out, he was glad for the haute

nard, the purificatory pedicure, sandal
season looming. O Summer, you are the nard

for the funk I'm sunk in. O, Summer, we throw
it all open for you expecting something new

when all we have inside is the same old self.
It's wild how easy going seems. Cut off

a tomato's toe and soon, from its bedhead
comes fruit for your bacon and white bread.

You can try it from seed, but taproots are prone
to Daddy issues. O Summer, you wade in

so shallow, but when you go, the drain is deep.
Maybe this is just an odd afternoon, a little life

and what, other than a moth-eaten sweater
do I know of sheep? No more than I know

of Martians, little green men in saucers
with suckers and feelers and sensilla

who may want to dominate me or digest me.
O, Summer, how do you manage it?

The coming and going and coming back
to where you've been? The gazing and grazing

of all the woolly ewes, lame rams, sad lambs?
Sure, you can call me a shepherdess, I guess.

This is clearly my crook, my broke herd song.

Soul Train

Who am I so small to wear big earrings? Bigger than my ears. Bigger than my stomach. Bigger than my birthday.

When June comes, I'll (1) eat all the letters until I'm fat-brained (2) play Uncle Bub's harmonica until my lips can ride a Huffy into town, alone (3) buy up all the magazines with things that don't belong and hidden objects which usually include an earring, small, in clouds or bushes (4) cut out the moon and paste it on my blue pages and shape up silver hoops from oven wrap and dress up the moon like a rich lady who goes to Mozart music with red chairs where there are naked statues of gold women that I can't help staring at, statue women who wear all the big earrings they want with their hair piled high in heavy loops or swimming down their backs wearing just earrings and nothing else so no one even notices the earrings or notices nothing but the earrings.

P. S. Ears are the best parts to decorate, better than fingers or necks or even ankles and I tried ankles with an angel on a gold chain that pierced the spine of my ankle so I broke it off and put it in the ash at the bottom of the burn barrel to see how long it would last, to see if angels are real.

P. P. S. Maybe in June I'll also (5) practice singing until everyone who goes by my house says:
> "There lives a girl who is like a bushel light and one day, one day she is going to dance into our living room singing, probably wearing the biggest earrings we've ever seen probably bigger than a tambourine or the TV or that old picture of gold angels hanging over the TV probably her voice will make us feel like we're standing on the edge of a waterfall preparing to jump
>
> or even better like we did
> and as we splash into
> a disco ball, we turn

gold and just as we
pop up to take a breath
two big birds
of paradise fly
close enough
to brush
our cheeks."

Obit: Ingénue, fleur terne

She was blindsided by an ice cream truck roller-skating home from the deep end in her pom-poms. She was sunburnt. Neighborhood kids rescued choco-locomotives and razzleberry-rockets, so all was not lost. Her body was reassembled with botox, implants, and glitter glue. She was dressed in a dreamgirl babydoll and laid on a picnic table at a rest stop after everyone left. Visitations will be held every sunset at baby Jesus stay-away camp where games and journal writing in trees will occur according to the big hand. It's important to write ingenuously for 5 minutes about how she trusted people—cads, father figures, heroes, who let her down, about how she wasn't all that candid or virtuous herself, about how she let herself down, all the plots she saw, heard, tasted, and contrived. #2's provided. Be sure not to stop writing until you hear stop. Contrived may seem hardest until you realize bags of douche often win, until you realize the time has come to fork your tongue. Just write what you feel. If all you feel is the weight of diminution, write about the shrinking arts, how the fetishism of doe eyes feels, the pressing and pressing and pressing of nails, the wasting of a waist, the shrinky dinky doo of a voice, the chipping away of what I say, the inventory of parts, the melting and hardening of the Madonna-whore-girl-next-door. Time will be provided for sharing. Keep in mind, men have always scooped out subdued brains like sorbet lest they think—always used the rootcaps of beings like

Ingénue for soup or blooms or stock, as a demonstrative curtain call for the mongerdrama—just capture that. In lieu of flowers, wear your tits out and pasties made from asters and a tutu or muumuu, hard-boil your boots, be prepared to heave, but keep your head about you. Masks may be dropped in the casket or the grave. Be sure to sign the guestbook with one wish. Be as ambiguous as you please. Animal crackers and cartons of milk with missing kids will be shared. In lieu of a procession, attendees are exhorted to vamp it up in the empty platter parade. Ingénue's epitaph will read:
Suit yourself.

Desire

A doe with glammy eyes
high steps through the yard toward
the remains of an eviscerated pumpkin
abandoned in the Pachysandra.

Through the window, I see her
and recognize the hunger for more
than a few clingy green leaves
in a seedy world full of orangeness.

Any Relationship With Light Is Complicated

When light left the first time
       I should have seen dark disrobing.
I learned early to love shadows.
       They leave a lot to be desired
and this is in line with what I want
       out of living. They also do wonders
for my Polish nose and slivers of Ice Age
       lip. I kept busy playing lady-on-a-scooter
with headscarves to die for.

When light left the second time
       despair seduced me, so I shot
myself at meteorically strange dudes
       with cavelike chests I could crawl into
to drink, grow pale, and get tattoos.
       For example, the sullen boy who played
piano in the shadow of Chopin's nose.
       Thank God for the girth of it,
serenades get garish fast.

When light left the third time
       I heard Chopin didn't live long.
His mazurkas, though, lived on in my
       grandma's paczki. Funny, Frédéric
François and Frances both lived
       in the umbra of organs and died
with flaming hearts. A lot desired always
       expires romantically—picture a black
Vespa in the mist, a silk scarlet scarf
       poofing over the ocean.

Finally, I realized romance is a scam, so
       I stopped counting light's comings/goings.
I recommend it. Light goes, let it go.
       When it goes, mazurkas are composed

in kitchens, like my grandma Fran's, who loved
        to polka while her hair set and she went
about using up whatever she had
        before it spoiled, as folks have since
medieval times—dark ages.

And what's berserk is whatever oven
        I was born with my head in
has nighted me with a wild, ferocious desire
        for a lot left to be desired.
Finally, I learned to tuck into my own cave
        nestled in my own craggy ribcage where I
scoot along, chiffon tied under my chin
        tasting the apricot moon, my mouth
blinking like a hazard light on a hairpin
        turn in the cliff face.

POP Swatch From Dug Up Miniature Lane Cedar Box

Eight face guards + One cracked face + Two damaged hands + Six replacement bands + Twelve disposable camera selfies + Seven problems makeup and lighting can't fix circled with cherry chapstick = a Picasso-like face, said a boy in history class

It's taken almost fifty years, seven homes, two marriages, four miscarriages, one motherhood, a couple of Gods, countless jobs, two and a 'half diagnosed disorders, three degrees of demarcation, lots of Mayzie fantasies, an epic splitting, a real zero self, and a zillion popified anodyne pill peddlers, in one dank junk-bunk after another, to get my hands on a decent kitchen knife, but finally I feel like Picasso must have felt holding a brush, holding my knife

In no time flat, I can cut the eyes out of potatoes and embalm the remains. It's an old wives' tale, but I put potato slices in my socks to suck up toxins while I dream of symmetrical shapes and a man, eating carpaccio, being run over by a blue Pinto. Every time the Pinto hits him, he spins 'round like a faceless foosball dude on a rod, a flap of raw meat splats the windshield to the click-clack click-clack of an abacus—what a game, what a pilot light

I can admit, I was the girl before a mirror, but now I am the woman with flower, the woman with book, and from time to time, I am the butterfly alight on that boy's eyeball that keeps him tossing on his vinyl mattress swatting at his face because I do like to think of myself as untitled, a little fractured in space, shape-shifty, and nude in a garden, not unlike the spiney poems tucked under the abstract geometric bands locked in my chest

To the Wives/Girlfriends of My Old Boyfriends

My father broke bones trying to play basketball
with the boys who kept coming 'round full of
hope and hormones at a time when the only
thing that interested me
about them was their longing. He laced up
his All-Stars and longed for a layup
in the community park before giving the boys
cause to say oh no in a way that meant
some ways of getting old are better
than other ways of getting old. So if you see I've
been poking around you on socials — look, if I'm
lurking, it is with longing but not for what you
have or what I had
or don't or how he is or isn't or what was
or could have been, what all-star kids you have
or haven't, how your stomach looks
by the ocean, or if you've held yourself up
higher or lower than I have to the bar rail
whether you dress up or undress
or dress down what the boys who hung around
your home came for or what score you keep on
your calendar.
I am a woman now as you are a woman now.
I understand the longing of a man
is the longing of a man as you understand
the longing of a man is the longing of a man so it
is you and I that have something
in common, something that has nothing
to do with longing for a man.
What I long for as I drive by
what's left of the basketball court across
from the dead end, just as I drive by you
are the fragments of me
that might got buried there.
You may understand this longing backward
to say oh no in a way that means
this way of getting old is better
than any man.

The Vagina Poem
—with homage to Georgia O'Keeffe

The earth has a vagina

It is the grandest canyon in existence, of existence, about existence
astride, prior to, but, of course

Vaginas are evolutionary, consider the timeline
sacrificial virgins to sensational monologues
to schmaltzy Gwyneth candles and Spencer's candy dishes

Vaginas have smoked cigars after George Sand
invoked cigars after Yes, We Can
given cigar testimony in Monica's hands

So many vagina battlefields, Kellerman's daring dive
O'Keeffe's red cannas, Pamela's honeymoon
to name a few, have been historically preserved

Amidst the slaying of Roe vs Wade
and gender-affirming bill bans

Linguists who wax poetic about semantic shifts
might remind us slay means to kill violently, wantonly
in great numbers

And to delight, impress, amuse

Of course, to adjudicate meaning, it's the context we use

To decide how we should respond to the men outside
the meat market bouncing baby killer signs

If vaginas were steering wheels, we might do well
to remember the 10 & 2 rule is démodé
downright dangerous today

According to horny boys, vaginas are like apple pies

Pies of all kinds are prescribed for posterity in *American Cookery*,
the first kitchen compendium in the USA

With this keeper for pioneer vaginas: "rules and maxims
that have stood the test of ages will forever establish
the female character"

Vaginas in need of dictation indeed

Vagina is a word governing relationships
best managed with some elasticity

Like Silly Putty, James Wright's baby
not James Wright whose women drown every evening
in Wheeling

But GE engineer James Wright who was trying to invent
a rubber substitute for American boys at war

He called it Nutty Putty
It's still sold in an egg

Lately, my vagina's grown restless and I'm wondering
if the Earth's might have sage wisdom

So I've taken compassionate leave and rented
a mule

A resolute, unimpregnable, sure-footed mule to go deep
into our geogenic wonder

To discover egg-laying bone beds, to better understand
what ages of pressure and cutting
circa exposure, erosion, collision
affect or effect

And to put to bed all of the associations with vaginas
hung on my vagina

For instance, how you think I think about vaginas
like you do, how you think I see vaginas
like you do

So you can do with my vagina like you would do

Nuts, amirite

My stay has been okayed by the Major Body herself

That is, as long as I love the place
and leave no trace

Day Breaks

Every day the sun goes away   it has other places to be
other people who need it   think much about it

Dark is worth its weight   it takes three days
in absolute darkness   to stop worrying   about making sense

Light is the greatest generation   fire more about hunger & heat
Light's mum, but   so savage   so fragile   and ravishing

Edison said   he ransacked the world to make it
That was probably more about the man   but

caught me   because I ransack best without light
Earth's face   is a real Wooly Willy

An every day face can   without warning   call off everyday
Relationships   predate faces

Bee balm, mums, campanulas, daylilies, yarrow   anything
bulbous or fibrous   easily uproots and splits

I wonder out of 100 people   how many know
what a campanula is   I'll confess I don't know

what it means to know   which is in direct proportion   to light
and dark   I wonder out of 100 people   how many know

what it means to camp   out of that number
I wonder how many have been camping   of those

I wonder how many would say   they love to camp
and in that group   I wonder how many

actually do   love it   if I have a point   it is that
Firstly, I kept putting my hands   on my cheeks

because I felt   alone at home   curling
my fingers in front of my eyes   to catch the moon

Soon, my armpits grew damp   so I laid down on dirt
and the daredevil took my air   dirt spewing everywhere

Firstly is ridiculous   take first love, for instance
It's not love at all   but a palmar reflex   a spoon to grasp

On my bucket list   something we say because it's dark   to say
I'm going to die   is to take in the Northern Lights

A breathtaking reminder   that the hangover only strikes
after day breaks   up an explosive, electrifying night

Infusion

Blood has soaked my arm and drips
down the side of the chair
that sounds like a boat.
   The nurse says sorry and thanks a blonde
   for the cookies. *Hope you like them,* the blonde
   says, *they're from Bite Me,* she says
   I love it down there.
      Down on Water Street, she means, where James Wright's
      golden-hearted whores used to drift around darkened doors.
      Sorry the nurse says, again, smearing blood all over my arm
      as the blonde turns on Fox News saying,
      Will it bother you.
      I feel a little floaty, as in out-to-sea, honestly, and I
      think about that village on the Amalfi Coast
      where the Theoi Halioi, barefoot, gathered their little wooden
      boats, lined up like Necco Wafers, early in the morning
      the sound of rope dragging and dropping
   rocking and creaking and how they gave me
   a sure vibe they could never be bothered, something
   they seemed to learn from the fish
   even the dying ones
that would, before day's end, melt on someone's
tongue like first fish, last fish too.

The gulls, though, and all the little birds with sticklike
            legs and needle beaks, they seemed intensely
                        bothered by everything.

Severstal Re-Opens the Yorkville Plant in Time for Christmas

My father worked, when he wasn't
laid off, for Wheeling-Pittsburgh Steel.
He wrapped leftovers in silver paper
and carried a Char-Vac and promised
to take me 100 feet up inside his crane
cab to see the mammoth fires that raged
below him as he sat on an inflatable
orthopedic donut and showed me
while cranking the window on our beater
how his knuckles were becoming cyclopean
and told me about savage one-eyed monsters
and made me listen to Mad Dogs & Englishmen,
Pearl, and Shakespeare's green-eyed monster
on vinyl and his buddy (he always had a buddy
doing this or that) sing *Knock, Knock, Knocking
on Heaven's Door* on cassette tape for months
on end riding along Rte. 2. Along Rte. 2 at night
the mills looked like storybook forests thousands
of gold lights plunging in and bursting out
of the river while monolithic machines pressed
ingots by forcing impurities to the top
of molten steel and out of nowhere walking
through a hotel lobby last winter in Lake Placid
my arm brushed a man's blue blazer
and it smoldered.

Just in Case the Other 49 States Wonder How We Write Poems in WV, or How We Write Poems in WV, or We Write Poems in WV

We grow things.
We break what we grow.
We throw things.
We don't throw things away.
We take back what is taken.
We let nature give and take us.
We make silence sacred.
We avoid vagueness like the plague.
We cozy up with wild, put blackberries
on our cheeks and feed Auntie Fern's
squirrel stew to lyrics, mystics, Salvadors, and socialites.
We start with stereotypes like the one
in Mel Brooks's *History of the World: Part II*
because writing a poem in WV
is worse than going to hell in bare feet
where *Country Roads* karaoke loops on hell's bells
and 16 tons of smoked roadkill w/ramp jelly
is served in sulfur clouds by carbide helmet lamp
by Don Knotts lookalikes, not to mention
the exhibitions and I don't mean sawtooth
self-immolations and serpentine flagellations
no, I mean rednecks and hillbillies and yahoos
and bumpkins in jacked-up trucks, country cousins
white trash, fiddle'n-'n'-moonshinin' yokels
Gee-gaws and pawpaw Pa-paws
hogwallers in the mountains, hills, and hollers
hollerin' bout coal stoves and missing teeth
like Anse Bundren, like Old Devil Anse
like Devil Went Down to Georgia, like coal miner's
daughter, like she asked for it, like daddy's
drunk in Daisy Duke's doublewide, like stand by
whatever ole man, like feuds and flags, seceded
suck it up, mustard seeds, hayseeds, hemmed, hawed

and all the g's got washed up. We think
about what my mother said: *We ain't the South.*
We reckon our hearts don't frack differen'
yours—you sing canary, carpetbagger!
We patch our holey gut buckets, black lungs, broken backs.
We hold up a match. We fan the flames. We bless your heart
with our burn barrel, our goodest book.
We clumb our catharsis like blue-jawed pioneers
and like molten steel we get our hope good 'n hot
and we worsh mud so free a'the flaps
y'all 'll want to come to podunk 4-wheelin 'n panhandlin
but be aware, beware, we traverse mountains
and refill our pens in the dead of night
with all manner of almost heavenly light.

lunch? (i wanted to say beautiful)

because we share washing sheets
warm alarms tender showers
                  undercover
                  sleepyhead
because plain skin is a shrine
skin to skin a salve
                  mattress sag
                  rescued dog
because I have just learned
of Robinson Jeffers' inhumanism
                  astonishing
                  pistachio shells
because I have lived unbeautifully
like a bulging vulture
                  bone breaking
                  beak
because the glue of you découpages
my papier-mâché soul
                  authentic
                  umbrella
because I understand Fay Wray
feared her pounding chest, more
                  hairy ape wrap
                  mango chutney
because I am terrified of squeezing it
—tender—to death
                  wild gutting
                  whoa co-op
because a blind man in the market
covers Journey songs
                  keyboard
                  sewer grate
because here's a swan
this is not a park
                  superfreaky
                  heady love

Bat in the Wine Rack

We kill it. Especially as adolescents,
they get confused. We dump it
into what's left of the hostas.
It's easy to forget we're animals.
It's easy to hide in athleisure wear.
We don't know which of the thirteen
native species it represents.
I want to believe it has pink lips
he says white nose.
I want to believe it's up from Hellhole.
He says we didn't want to.
It's not like we wanted to,
but we all get curious about death's
Rolodex effect. I understand
a backhand. We're all part
of some racket. Consider the functional
nature of an umbrella, whether weather
is unpredictable anymore, and how
many ways a body can be trapped.
I make devil's food cake.
We sit by the firepit.
We get eaten alive.
We sleep in smoke.
He takes the remaining cake to work.
I clean out my son's closet,
who is somewhere holding himself
together, I hope.

III

To feel shame is to feel seen, acutely diminished.

—Kaufman

Advice for the naked baby I found in the snow

Get some clothes.

You'll probably need a mother
for this—the woman in a blue, weather-resistant
coat might be an option. I don't want to
get metaphysical—you're too infant
but she appeared out of whiteness
at precisely the moment I stooped
to dislodge you from a packed track
of dirty snow.

She came to you.
She laid you out in her bare palm,
she knew how to do that—
her eyes knew what to look for.
She used a milky sip of fingernail
to scrape the dirt from between your legs,
the crease of your lips.

I never saw pink until I saw you
in her palm—your blossom-flesh
against one of her leaves
still photosynthesizing.
Her roots are strong!
She has named you already
King.

She knows that you come from
where two leavened ends meet
and that you bring cause to celebrate.
You'll need a mother like this—
a mother aware of her privilege
and obligation.

Antimother

Her womb was saddled with wanderlust.
Lacking convention, perhaps conviction, it was colonized
by worms, but when the time came, her womb came home.
A battleship? Sunken a little? But, her womb came home
dragging its dinghy. Her womb came back
like a whale slapping its tail. Her womb came home
sepia, soft and glistening like a head of roasted garlic.
Her womb came home sawed-off, dangling
like balls from a truck hitch. Her womb came home
hirsute like Hendrix, hands on fire. Her womb came back
playing Black Bear on bagpipes for the orphaned organs
plagued by bad breaks. Her womb came back
to its captor with a handful of dandelions. Her womb came home
to her lips she can't keep stitched. Her womb came home
to her abdomen, a tangled mangrove, to her eggs hanging
their cockles in the gestational cloakroom.
But her womb came home to call it quits, to stop pretending
it isn't pedestrian and terrestrial.

She left the bottom half of the Dutch door unlatched
for her prodigal, home for good this time
from the lounge and the piano by the sea.
She's finally starting to see her womb as all grown up.
Now that her womb's home she can nurture her womb
in the kitchen, the heart of the home.

Her womb makes room for nurturing. Her womb stops
affecting beatific light. Her womb starts deadlifting.
Her womb opens itself, emancipates, delivers the anguish
it couldn't shake as mistakes, shakes the pillars
collapses the temple. Finally maybe baby only lonely
unconditionally lovely beastly fully languidly
flappingly freely freely her womb pays rent.

Immodest Proposal

I.   Background

     This girl had a small life of small things
     smelly stickers, jelly shoes
     and from time to time a mother
     who left candy on her pillow
     to let her know, yes this thing
     is full of jawbreaking things
     but also, from time to time, sweet things
     small things
     and from time to time, things
     small and sweet appear like things
     out of nowhere. Learn to listen to things
     and you will hear things
     expanding even as things
     dissolve on your tongue:
     a pretzel thing
     water fountain
     turtle and circus seal cement things
     a towering red thing
     a blinding silver thing
     that pares girls to things.

II.   Objective

     Devour your child—eat.
     Either the woman eats
     the girl or the girl eats
     the woman. Eat
     with your preying manus, eat
     her mouth with drawn butter, eat
     every last gash with gusto. Eat
     her heart until it quits beating.
     Scorch her and your roof with heat.

III. Scope

Picture ghost peppers holding
tapers, those little Sunday school candles held
under cardboard cuffs. Hold up
your eyes to the flame and sing for your supper
This Little Light of Mine.

There are more than 7,000 varieties of apple
forever laced with sin. Gut her and stuff her with apples
Honeygold and Red Delicious.

IV. Plan/Budget

Forgive yourself. I do.
That's a lie. I do
not. I do not listen well, either.
Listening to the mystics do
mystical, all I do
is hear girls done
on spits, sugarcoats blistering. Yes, I did
smack my lips fat melting.
A woman pays for what she does
not eat and for what she does.

La Mirada Fuerte

Nothing in the mirror
Nothing going according to plan
Nothing going the way of geese
Nothing in the determined shape of an arrowhead
Nothing forward in its motion
Nothing with a warmer destination in mind
Nothing banking on arctic exploration, either, suggestive of survival
Nothing of creation which is really just survival by another name
Nothing diminutive like Maggie or Peggy for Margaret
Nothing of Frankenstein who was actually the doctor
And nothing of the monster
And monster is nothing but another name for creation, a pet name
    like hubby or veggie or knock-knocks for Pa-Paw for toots-a-loo
Nothing beating inside the heart of the monster made it a monster
It was a human heart after all
Nothing is spared from miscreation
Nothing miscreated escapes framing—the swollen-headed girl
    made the corn grow
Nothing is made too delicate to be destructive—consider mosquitoes
Nothing reminds me so much of delicacy as a winter day sipping
    snow from bone china
Nothing as pitchfork and mob as light
Nothing as savage as stillness
Nothing as monstrous as beauty
Nothing more devastating than monsters who see themselves
    in everything
Nothing so presumptuous as believing yourself human

ENG AP

My feet on the book rack under the desk
under a wide-necked kid who holds on to numbers
and dumbells in his annals. We exist to each other.
I have no idea what a Tippet is.

It's become clear the pin oak I dialogue with from my bathroom
window is allegorical. It holds on to its dead in the same way
I thought I needed to keep my mother's body, not ironically,
in a spare room.

Mrs. Moore is talking about mortality and grief. I never bought
the whole burial imagery, I guess. Taxidermy is a better
perspective. At that point, hollowing out becomes personification.

We don't have to follow food anymore, so why not advance the plot?
We could have dead rooms for the preservation of families.
Wait. Too late, thanks to Hitchcock, who abused the whole
Mother apostrophe—now it just seems silly.

It's not my bathroom. It's just some exposition to establish
myself. Space would become an issue, but then it already has.
I'm supposed to be thinking about dead Emily Dickinson (exhausting)
and em dashes, talk about holding on.

The energy I give to fighting with Emily is vulgar.
I assumed em dashes were Emily's namesake rather than
a practical function of print. Em dashes & Emily, a story
we tell about a story she told herself.

I'm teetering, swept into an attic, a shopworn space for weird
dead ~~moms~~ dolls. It's me though, lying on an—in an awful shawl.
It's my mouth, the long, flat line trying to hold on
to something like the branches of the pin oak—this metaphor
signifies Bildungsroman.

The hall pass is a hunk of driftwood. In the bathroom stall
hyperventilating, I wonder about Mr. Whipple's backstory.
What made him so averse to squeezing softness?

what I did this summer

learned i'm a hive / made the dog's head into a tepee

grew quiet / wrote my name with leaves, twigs, bones, feathers

pored over wild blackberries / crawled through tunnels no taller

    than my knees

        to see how my body understands underground

took up with night to study dark lives and star sleight of hand

    to figure out how stars coax hope from tombs

embraced mountains to enlarge my embrace / let my soul

    hitchhike, a little

        to collect dust in outer space

calculated the cost of storms caused by waspishness / measured

        clouds based on loss

slept with salt in my wounds / ate from sea swells / scrubbed

    my lips with sugar

put my ears to my cells to chart vibrations / gave away shots of royal jelly

    to everyone hard at work being

chaised in new cells

got blubber-lipped by the beeyard abloom / savored every flavor

    of Twin-Pop back-to-back

no one called my name

        not once

Goose is Still Dead, Maverick Comes Back to Teach

Just want you to know there's a *Top Gun* sequel
that's got you written all over it.

Who can forget how you cried over Goose
for weeks until it got really weird.

Goose has a son, Rooster, in this one. Remember
the rooster your dad got before we even knew

about egg danger zones, the rooster that woke us
to the terrible celerity of mornings.

I heard your dad finished that old Plymouth,
heard it's red and running. I can't picture it though

off the blocks. My son got a touch lamp at Goodwill
and I remembered our SOS system, the one we made

to say *hi* and *I'm going to bed* from my dead end
to your exit when the dark could take

our breath away, when we had no idea
what was worth saving and couldn't stop talking

about everything we'd leave behind. Thought
you'd want to know, no one dies in this one.

It's one of those sellout endings. As a matter of fact,
it's a replication—a pattern match. Remember

tracing paper and how I copied all your people
because I could never get people right

—huge heads, lopsided legs, fused fingers, anyway
it's like that, except at the end, every great ball of fire's

been diffused, it's just a bunch of buzzing the tower
at dusk, like that time I visited you with chocolate milk

and Tigerbeat and we watched as they launched
balloons outside the window of your hospital room, but

also, we kind of recognize now how balloons are no good
for the environment. Not that someone has to die.

Backscratcher

How miraculous to extend my reach
to help me reach parts of myself
I can't otherwise reach. It's difficult
to reach yourself, let alone anyone else.
Truth is clammy, clumpy, clampy.
There's an etching on the handle, almost
like a birthmark or burn, with Japanese characters
I can't grasp. Maybe they're cherry blossoms?
I lost Christmas one year, there was a fall
right into spring. Thereafter, I lost
one family but found some odds 'n' ends
action figures, doll heads and limbs
in a bargain bin at Hobby Lobby, so I crafted
another one full of prosthetics, exotics
and eccentrics, a mutt too. We live in a watercolor
toybox with Sharpie graffiti. It's just how
I imagined life. My new family talks a lot
about cupolas and superglue and we've acquired
quite a collection of autographed and inscribed
bibles, same way people collect vintage ads,
Life magazines, state spoons, torn balloons,
dashed hopes, or family history they plan
to scratch. Hey, they say Gideon's Bibles
were the brainchild of traveling salesmen
who preached, from Superior, Wisconsin,
we should focus on who we are
before God. Turns out, Gideon
was just another obedient disciple, just
another tray of cold cuts on Christmas Eve.
I recall one Christmas, my old dad
gave my old mom *The White Album*
and I remember that fuzzy hug
of the needle drop and wondering
how anyone could live without that.

Consumer Alert: Mariah Carey

Everything you consume affects your sex life.
But that's part of the problem, isn't it?
We mistake it all for Christmas.

Many new years from now, I may forgive
our insatiable desire for icicles—lametta
the Italians say, meaning tiny blades.

Marvelous for cutting out darling, holy tide
baubles of adoration and futzing
with facial deconstruction.

It occurs to me we're all part of the Potato Head
family, roots dangling, obviously, from our eyes
cheeks contoured with nightshade.

I feel safe in the dirt. I exude cold, dark.
Did you know mistletoe is parasitic?
But that's part of the problem, isn't it?

You're more the basking type—always
looking for light right outside your door.
Basking grows banal.

I've heard the North Star is a conspiracy.
The Pope said no nativity will give up
its donkey.

Especially if Jesus is waiting to judge us, I want
a donkey laying among me and you are more
the stable ox.

Your face reminds me of a throne, though
the way your cheekbones sit so high
and look like hay in a manger.

For the specious present, I haven't deleted your almighty,
far away from this place face. Your birthday.
The date of our first getaway date.

Remember you got up in the middle
of the night to pee, slipped on the wet floor
chipped your teeth and blamed me.

It was probably my fault. I'm careless a lot.
And find holding on tight to be blizzard-like.
But that's the problem, isn't it?

Nevertheless, I'm going to keep you under
favorites for a while. But get on with your life.
Maybe each new year before

the tree comes down, I'll sit under it
for a minute to catch a final whiff
and pull you up under the pine

as a little counter-magic for the one
I really need, but that's part
of the problem, isn't it?

some rare but serious side effects may include

she's thinking in the dark
(dark is for thinking)
about how she hasn't felt a thing
today she'd like to blame the gynecologist

first thing Monday morning:
how was *your* weekend?
(Monday firsts are for thinking things)
 terrible, we found out a(nother) *friend*
has (another terrible) *Lou Gehrig's* (disease),
just spent a lot of time crying theDirectorofPR&Marketing said
she keeps a tumored dog in diapers
he still seems to enjoy life
she can't bear to put him down

it may have been raining
(rain is for thinking)
when she walked across Main Street to
pay Susan's lunch tab at *The S-Bridge,*
a slab of meatloaf w/o bread and a D.Coke w/ ice
the owner, George D., sat
in a booth cigar smoking,
figuring on green ledger pages

her husband's 34th birthday
cake, w/sweet icing, song sung and a pause
before blowing out the candle-
two wrought iron plant holders w/fleur de lis designs
Brad Paisley CD—boy from a neighboring town made good—
they're intellectual enough to mock country music
(country music is not for thinking)
but anti-pretense enough
to embrace their cultural heritage

her son climbs into the shower
(showers are for thinking)
she smooths coconut scented shampoo over
his scalp, he clasps two large, less-than-plastic gems
from a goodie bag his littlebuddy brought back
from Disney World's Pirates of the Caribbean,
the orange one, he explains, doesn't have any special powers
it's just dead, maybe from too much wishing

but she can't explain to a medical doctor
(medical doctors are for thinking)
that shethinks-shewants his little t-shaped plastic stick
removed because she hasn't felt a thing
in a long time,
maybe since he embedded it in her uterus

Well

—[WV] *State law requires that operators disclose the chemicals used in hydraulic fracturing, but exceptions can be made which allow these chemicals to be concealed from the public.*

Well, well, well
When someone asks how you are
the school marms urban dictionary identifies
as bespectacled virgins, old and stingy, fond of floral print granny
panties say it is grammatically accurate to identify
yourself as well

If you are indeed well, honestly
it's probably best to say you are well
even when you are not well
because everyone has something to be
unwell about, so telling someone
who's noways well
that you are actually unwell may shore up
their overall sense of
unwellitude

You must know, whether you see the operating lights
from your back bedroom
parked by the geese-mossy lake
through purple flowers hanging like poultices over lattices
over lovers over joggers over dogs
whether you hear the ground groaning
with split ribs
fractured collar

You must know, whether you Ascend WV for $12,000 in cash,
no strings attached or trace your Pappy back
to the bed, bank, and shores of the Ohio River
or so much of Big Sandy, river of sandbars
when someone asks how you are
you dig deep
you wish
you say well

Why I Love (Even Lame) Graffiti

Place, she said, must crack
—for affectivity, she meant.
I stand on the ruins of a fort
where a Chieftain stands
with his hand raised to say
what they want him to say.
He stands bronze on the spot
where they say McColloch leapt
into a crack by the river
and survived broken bones
though his horse did not.
Where we ate square pizza
with cold cheese and chugged
Boone's Farm, where we discovered
love sprayed wildstyle and left
our underwear under the back
seat, where we went to thread
the baubles of our dead on knotted
twine or braided twigs and totter
along the retaining wall to throw moon
shots over the hill toward Short Creek.

You, I say, must break
to find the hidden strength
of a place. You must crack
your ribs and admit a place
just as the roller rink
and city pool opened
their gates every Sunday
for the poor kids
to skate when it was cold
and cool down in the heat.

Vp of Women Against the Collapse of Our Civilization Coalition or Fleet Supervisor for Car Wraps as a Means of Finding Your Tribe in a State That Bottom Ranks on Most Lists: Economy, Employment, Education, Health, and Straight, Flat Thoroughfares

heretofore not civic or always civil or sure to which civilization
I belong while buying toilet paper
at Dollar General I am reminded
by a woman not from WV, shoelaces woven
through her gray braids, who follows me home
because I have 35 bumper stickers
on my VW from places not WV
that civilizations have ended
—collapsed—
permanently closed their doors
like the monolithic malls of my childhood
where girls like me first tasted freedom
sweet as Cinnabon, substantial as a Sbarro's slice
dark as Carmike Cinemas' late show
and as far as she can see, we bought the chokers of ruin
from Claire's
—BOGO—
she is not worried for herself
but for her grandchildren, her international heifers, and her son
in Sonoma, she wants to know if I have been to those places
plastered across the trunk of my bug
those places that are anywhere but WV
as though it's an interview in the driveway
of my suburban home
for a job though I don't know what

Laundry

is what I'm doing
laundry and I'm pulling my hair out
thinking about moon
poking me in the eye
floating behind my tufted head
thinking I should pierce
my face to let moon know
I don't need it
that I can phase it out
that I can make my own light
that cows want to jump over me
that I have some pull over the tide
that I can pierce, too
that I can gauge and stud
my eyes, lips, tongue, and septum
that I can pull off snakebites and angel eyes
that I can swing a sickle
that I can cast a gold shiv
into the innermost chamber
of a human heart and stalk
the darkest brush inside
a thumping chest like a leopard
invisible to the naked eye
and clamp my jaw on an elegant
antelope's throat and drag it
limp, up the brainstem
into the amygdala of a selenophile
then rest my head against
what I had to kill
what I need to clean
and I'm listening to bleach scream
and scooping damp sweatpants
and razorback tanks and leopard
print thongs out of a broken dryer—okay
okay, maybe it's time to throw in the towels

maybe I do need moon, maybe I need moon
to smear love on the lonely
lost sock of my soul

Movie at the Waterfront

Dogs curl up at her feet
like pill bugs. She knows
what it's like to bury
yourself. The small one
quivers as small things settled
into the palm of this world
often do. She knows what it's like
to be destructive too.
A large man with a small
mouth speaks to his shoes
like he's staring down
a no-fall zone. The dogs
are too old for save-the-day
seductions—they care
about rescue only as it relates
to hunger. They are beholden
to late-day yawn and stretch
on these, their days
just as she has reached
an age (it is singularly something
to say an age has been reached)
when people are prone
to say she came to it late
whatever it may be, in this case
watching *Jaws* for the first time
though it was released
the same year she was
dangled by her feet.

At the Lake

The Greeks thought we were the center of the universe
until Copernicus, with his Polish nose squarely in the center
of his face, bouffant pageboy in orbit, came along
with his closet of baubles. In the next room, my son's friend
tells a girl in Texas he loves her. He climbs all over love
like monkeybars. The *I* and the *love* and the *you* hang
like soaked trunks over lamps, loungers, and balconies.
My husband with his cheaters perched on the tip
of his nose, his nose like a lone star, the two of us lying
like border states with mountains running through us
and a deep lake between us and this kinky old sun
always falling down; nonetheless, she keeps her face
painted, she's radiant, all waxy and dewy as she lets
her lux curls fall loose against our ankles, alongside
her tongue where sails melt like tablets. No one
bothers to ask about her dim view of orthodoxy
or the epochless cultivation of collapse all the water
people in their water towns won't own. Inevitably,
they keep their bodies hard and minds sharp gathering
gewgaws by the water. But, hey, look at me, puddle
of matter, absorbed in a brief history of humankind
as he drifts off. Isn't he a state of kindness?
I understand why Copernicus kept his heliocentricity
secret a while. My son's friend, still bobbing in the Loch
Ness of love, echoes the lake slapping drunk kisses
all over the rock face. Slowly things come around
to accept nature and history, the humanness of our kind.
Tomorrow, it will be time to pack up our makeshift
closets. What is a closet but an organization of space.
An intimate cosmos we create to create ourselves.
Where most of us have at least one pair of shoes
or pants we know we'll never wear again but
we won't let go of—we hold on to them anyway.
We even pack them and take them from place to place.

Every last thing was gold
—after Van Gogh, The Immersive Experience

but I feel dirty, Vincent, like I owe you
an apology, like maybe I slept with Gauguin
just the once, Absinthe and lonely, you understand
that dreadful nagging to levitate, to transcend
skinny jeans and mom jeans and pottery classes
and self-indulgence and sorrow, grown-up coloring books
the brow beatings over luminism
the way my spine has become a built-in sharpener
so yes, I was looking to be laid upon

gold

so I dawdled like a swan through the hay and wheat unfurling
almond blossoms, wide-brimmed hats, a postman's
mustache, prisoners spinning in halos
like post-menopausal women post-bottomless-mimosas
and yes, lazed in a starry, starry night
on the foreheads of strangers, and do you know
what I discovered? A girl turning cartwheels through cornfields
in my chest cavity who has never cooked a potato
never beat-the-clock with piss-warm drafts. She looked at me
and I looked at myself like she looked at me.
Vincent, that's an exhumation, but you understand
that kind of self-study, to cram and cram until
seeing what you need to see

gold

I know you understand because I studied you
studying yourself and to be frank, Vincent, it's no different
than the sad herd of us on Snapchat or IG. Can we not
take comfort, Vincent? The self endures the self.
Perhaps it's the only way to assure
we don't give up the search to be touched

gold

by the drag of your slipper, the free poster still rolled

gold

caked on my septum, you've made impasto of me
Vincent, a woman who keeps a girl trapped
in the file-out-through-the-gold-hustling-gift-shop
with posters already plastering the walls three-deep, Vincent
she has more chains than keys and nothing more
to study there, or buy. Vincent, she's ready for her release
her star, Vincent, just one.

gold

can you hear me?

Uvalde

My son is cutting grass.

I can see his lips moving along with whatever song
pumps into his head as he tries to perfect
the light and dark pattern in the grass.

He is about the same age in-between I was when my mother
threw a glass candy dish across the brown pall
of our living room, just missing my left cheek.

As I watched her pick up every shard of green coin glass
I could not imagine then the fear and sadness
always in her grasp.

I cannot imagine now the trampled lawns, blown glass, rage
too slick, hot, and sharp to touch, the mown patches
where nothing sweet is like to seed,
where so many hothouse hearts stopped, stopped
going great guns, stopped Texas cold.

Fresh Cut Grass Smell

When Joyce wrote the moo cow moos
well, it made all the sense I knew but didn't know
how to make, but now I cannot make sense of home
where I am confused because I'm not sure
whether I am there where I am always wondering
where I am.

I have made sadness make sense, though, I know.
I have made it into a sensible soup and used it to fill
a swimming pool too deep. I've let it settle like dust
on floorboards and blinds. I've collected it as moonily
as it collects Hummel figurines and I'm wondering
if I've made it home.

I also made myself a moony girl. I made myself a moony girl
who made too much of heavenly bodies, who tossed little boys
in craters, who blasphemed the lunar cycle, who smashed
her bedroom windows with broken brooms.
Until, I made a boy of my own, time for the girl to get lost.
Now, I may have lost the boy too.

I would make a lousy astrophysicist, though I wonder all the time
about my place in the universe, and yours for what it's worth.
Who knows who made the moon, but we make it mean something
every day. To make is to dissect moonstruck.

Just look at the blue tee-shirts, sunflower seeds, Hey Dudes
all moon-dewed, strewn all over a faceless room.
So I will feed the fish, practice waxing gibbous faces
and reenact eclipses. Isn't it funny they're called funeral
homes?

Thing is, it's spring. The windows are open all night and the moon
keeps climbing into bed with me, breathing heavily
smelling of fresh-cut grass. I think this house is made

of Colorforms, one red rectangle, a blue triangle, a small green square
an enormous yellow circle, clinging to a blackboard.

But a boy is an organic shape and his heart a magnetic force
a gravity that keeps everything in its place.

Mom, the moon says to me, I made a man for you
with a boy in it and I put him in the mountains.
I made the clouds magnets and I found a cow
roaming around lowing to jump over him
until some other cows find their way home.

Child Loving Deviant Meaning

—No particular poetic form is defined by the expression of love
between parent and child —Google

I am subject to change
Two girls eat up eye makeup

Their lowered hearts burn
until they raise their electric grass elegy
to bury dusty Anbu masks

My God Matthew McConaughey
preaches mean, mean it, meaning greenlights
while I Walmart

Here's what the people are saying to My God:
     dizzy chat
     distance between cornhole boards
     appetite crap
     drop the fake lawncare
     admit why you are Ada Limón loving lemons
     I'm a quarter quirky prison person

Matthew McConaughey, My God
has convincing down to alcohol poisoning
so we become:
     West Virginia exodus
     Jesus by Ada lyrics
     a flogging flower girl

My God never minds strewing petals of self-pardon
sabotaging chaps or Cowden disease
My God makes everything alright alright alright

A frozen shame face, everybody knows shark week
a child frozen in the frontispiece
an elephant's graveyard, grace, gravy baby

Let go of what was supposed to be, My God
says to me poser positive junk
open those wings near me

My life is a shelf or shelter
a pink eye picture, optical deep dive
facial familial degeneration
peak of summer pea-sized sty

My possessive determination
my naked baby clamors over clover
beware flesh-eating bacteria from clams
or is it oysters

I do not wish him kid
I do not wish him king
I did not wish him kind

There he is, there he was
a chunk of pink cake
a playful calf calendar
better hair than butter
holding a blue bucket sans sand
holding a black hole needed
like a hole in the head

Uncut grass, popeyed clover
hand over love over hand

Everything Shakespeare said becomes
what about the violet
what about the violet smells
to him as vitamin D deficiency

All these of God's daughters—
wasn't it supposed to be doth to me
wasn't it supposed to be I became
McDonald's fries smothered

IV

ADULTHOOD WITHOUT EQUAL POWER IS A SHAM[E].

—KAUFMAN

The Penis Poem

—and so the woman who writes cuts herself out a paper penis
—Hélène Cixous, *The Laugh of the Medusa*

Maybe I've been running with scissors too long

When I discovered my first penis, I kept it in my pocket
it understood this to mean I was in love

Penis, I've always thought of you as a cog rattle
a stickshift, that little thimble in Monopoly

Simple enough
but you fancy yourself profound

See yourself as an astronaut, a doomsday bunker

A badger, when you're feeling hard or tired of everything
being so hard, a burrowing mammal, a humble-bumble, stumbling
into the closest safe, soft spot to refocus

My mother and her friends made a crib mobile for me, a jiggling
ring of peni (oooh, hit that pseudo-Latin spot) that hung over
my flailing limbs until I grew strong enough to swat

A memento I kept to keep handing
down

As soon as my eyes opened, I studied the shape in wood
felt and lead

Like my soft spots, my mother is dead

Fortunately, we all start writing about our mother's death
soon after birth

Every penis ever made was made by a mother
but a penis does not a mother make, though
there is no separating them

It's a thorny jigsaw at best
that begets every game, every Wordle text

It's the anima apocalypse, a mother's death, note how
she storyboards you long after she's gone

But we've already heard the one about how her work
has been tediously obscured

Oh I fondly remember lining up the usual suspects
for sport—I fancied myself an umpire
an origamist right away

Reading aloud from all the Mary's until the penis heads
pulled themselves together, thought a little better
stood down

I fondly remember popping Jagged Little Pills
with all my friends because what every bitch needs is a penis
of her making—a pattern for smiling

Now our daughters call us angry
but we call that MacGuffin to task and pull out
our signed Woolf pact

Though fake eyelashes make me choleric
you should know this poem isn't going to meet your needs
because you expect too much

Sometimes, it's exhausting
Sometimes, it gets me down

That's one thing I admire about a penis, its particular
joie de vie, an ad infinitum energy, the ole' college try
Bloodless tuft or bust!

And as a penis-maker, I've thought about Jesus
having a penis which would basically be God's penis
a hard cataphatism to miss

A penis in a manger, it's a congenitally crooked scene of narrativity
but what can you expect from soi-disant wise men
banging on like bells to please themselves

I can't help feeling an older sentiment, sediment
room for digging holes to make you whole
a well of first-person pennies in me

A frame to stretch me, feathers, wells of ink, a palette
ribbon for my hair, a barbell
for my tongue, baton in my right palm

Still, do not mistake me for playing paper dolls
scissors are a pair of sharpened blades
that slide against each other

It's important to keep that in mind the next time
you hold one in your hand

Blow Town

All the big feelings are claiming space on
our tiny blue dot.

When you found that old house in the woods and
wondered if you'd fall through the floors.

You did and you didn't want to fall through
someone else's long gone. And you did.
And you didn't.

Get caught up in cataloging squishy, spongy, gooey
things because they cling
to your fingers, lips, gratifications.

Get caught up in Light left behind conspiring
to fall through you, paddling your little canoe
like a salmon to spawn.

Let me be clear: watch out for Light—she is gutting and flooding.
A noose of mesmerism.

The stars in a constellation aren't actually connected at all.
All these years, I fancied them cryptographs.

Wasn't there one about Elmer Fudd tearing up his contract
with Warner Bros because they never
not once let him kill the rabbit.

Bugs understood Acme life, carried himself
a carrot away.

All the same, all the big feelings are what's up in enlightenment
traveling through space like dynamite, changing
the mass of our planet.

Scrolling
—sinister side effects offered effectually aside

May
cause palms to palpitate—May
cause irregular heartbeat induced by
whisker fixation—May
cause enlarged tongue to piebald—May
cause eyeballs to gyrate—May
suppress vocal variations—May
result in clopping like a billygoat—May
suffer spells of gruffness—May
induce gephyrophobia—May
suffer formlessness and facelessness as a
result of face after face after face—May
compensate for the lack of a face
by buying a goat farm—May
promote goat yoga & make goat soap
which certain hippies claim cures
facelessness—May
milk an algorithm—May
grow a false goat's beard—May
expose rectangular pupils—May
elicit taboos and voodoo that intensify
tinnitus—May
get gargantuan teeth—May
rant about grolar bears & geeps—May
suffer severe brain grout and identity
sweats—May
hear God whistle in a goat's nose—May
promote karaoke with goats—May
take up the pan flute—May
become infested with ticks, lice, flies
flukes, fleas, or Satan—May
lay low in a grotto—May
induce mood swings and trigger achy
egos—May

cause delusions of teleportation—May
cause episodes of daimonic panic—May
lead to kidding—May
cause head-butting due to brain atrophy
and boredom—May
cause you to gobble garbage
collapse bridge-by-bridge
and be cannibalized by trolls

Still, Life

Exactly how it happens is hard to say.

A nude sprawls on a vermilion couch
sheets tacked up galore to set a scene
and a naked girl studies hair.

Saints hidden like Easter eggs in nipples
grapes, craniums, biscuits
quails, quince, and tureens.

Nude: *The soft existence of living things*
was documented in mud and sand
more than 700 million years ago.
Naked: *Some days are that way.*

They float together with all the drama
of an ocean. It's hard to look away.

Caught in a fisheye outside a glinty window
a couple of cardinals eat seeds, open and close
their wings, shudder a little, but never leave.

They have no choice but to make love
and plainly say how they'd like to be supported
when they grieve.

They routinely seek proof of marriage, apply
for home improvement loans and put the boy

(enter a boy with a basket of fish, a shimmering perch
over his head, chanting catch of the month) first.

They'll rally for the boy before dying.
The boy will fill out death decrees.

Captive animals never truly return to the wild,
but with good acrylics and a stroke of devotion,
still life stands the test of time.

Halfway to Where Life's Begun

For one week each year, we pretend to be lake people.
Heavy with Deet, we move into a souvenir photo frame.
We eat flamingo because you are what you eat.
We don't care that flamingos aren't lake birds.
We crave the smack of brine tang.
We wear parrots in the wake, before dry, or God forbid wet
macular degeneration reveals how manmade
our lives have become. Bird species are homogenizing.
We wear white rubber sandals in solidarity
and gin sigh well, still, they fly, mostly.
We talk flow with swaggy adolescents sailing
through existence on iridescent shells.
We tell our children they were not inflatables
but thrashed into our laps like spellbound fish
as we leaned ourselves like crucifixes against Adirondack chairs
to watch the sun melt all over the mountains.
We make out dragonflies are maenads and lose
our minds to trees that smell like sex.
We pretend to need Yetis and to be yetis
who would certainly, pseudo-scientifically
reside lakeside, to B1 with the cryptid family,
our existence anecdotal but unsubstantiated.
We report all missing trees. For affect, we kayak.
An ancient lawnmower perennially stuck in the mud
becomes a real watershed. We reflect stillness and nod
deeply at depth. We slide off our shorts and dive
as though nothing we can't see could hurt us.
There's a local pilsner on tap, a crisp apocatastasis.
They say in every body of water, a sunken ship
—whatever it was, we call it treasure.

Playing the Ingénue

I've always worn my heart on my sleeve
and now I'm wearing you in my abdomen, darling tumor
for whom I wore the red sweater in fourth grade
the one with a pattern of sheep, pallid
except for the clichéd ewe.
It was my favorite then and you are my favorite
now. In this soft room, pregnant
with pollen, darling tumor, don't I spoil you?
Bending at certain angles that I might
trace your form, keeping you supple
with champagne so you may suffuse. I lie hard
as winter earth to feel you pushing up
like a tulip. Ours is a biblical affair.
For you, I robe fresh bread in Irish butter
macerate berries and wait patiently for crème Fraiche
so we can pique-nique under stained glass
as the sun fades away.

We've no time to waste, darling.
A white-hot passion like ours is destined to consume.
You will be sectioned and I will not see you.
I trust you understand. God,
I love tragic you.
I wonder, are you in the shape of a minaudière or fleur-de-lis?
I do hope.

The Ass Poem

My husband notices the new style of yoga pants
that truss the roast like butcher's twine.

At the gym, my husband looks at women's asses
all the time, but so do I.

Some of the reasons we look are plain enough.
Some are more like a symbology of infinity

we may never understand, so I can hardly be upset
by this natural setup. A woman's ass

is loquacious in the manner of an astrologist, spouting
aphorisms with each squeeze, bon mots with every

squat, preciously quick with wisecracks, but
there's something else about a woman's ass

we chew on each time we eat. A woman's ass
(you'll laugh to smother the slow burn of this simple

truth) is a geography of the mind. When you see
satellite pictures of this gas and rock planet you imagine

your hands on it. There she stands, oops, she dropped
her keys, the quarter moon she was going to press

into your palm and you feel yourself pampered.
Our planet is banded with highwires.

Our hearts and minds like acrobats crossing
nets and ethers meant to keep us together, hoping

to seem strong and clever, hoping to be seen
to be seen lest we are a ball of charged yarn

for cosmic cats. But a woman's ass carries
an empyreal current, twitches with wavefunction.

A woman's ass, every woman's ass, any woman's ass
is a power pendulum. I can't speak for my husband

whose reasons are his own, probably well-known
but the way I watch a woman's ass is like an astronaut

tracking the steps to countdown, to a world of ass
space, a world of space for my ass, a world where

all women's asses are my ass and the other way 'round.
This reminds me that a red fox, in the wild, lives

between 2 - 4 years on average. Now and then
one wonders into my yard, usually in a dawn fog

vibrating with stillness, an impervious ember, tail
as thicc as foxy_mama_your name on your tongue

the color of summers you've shaped to remember
an August cobbler, yes, the color of a drop-ripe

peach, but don't you dare repeat it (peach)
because I want no part of that—that thing we do

how we reduce every inexplicable miracle, every
simple wonder to something simple-ton, something

giphy, something I ♥, something that's the butt
of every joke, instead of just leaving the red fox

stopped in the grass, stopping my heart, stopping
time, alone.

State Fossil

—We have to let them know this isn't the WV they think they know.
                                                    —Wheeling Mayor GE

Remains attest colossal sloths lived where I live.

Feuding continues over what county, what cave, but its name
is firm: Megalonyx Jeffersonii.

You've heard about Jefferson's cottonmouth,
how saltpeter preserves meat, makes steel, guns, fire
work. Salt holds water. Dandelions drop seeds.

Me? I am for the distillation of dreams.

Maybe you've heard of Ralph Pierre LaCock, Pete Marshall
per Hollywood Squares, who lives, per this poem, in California
with wife #3.

My mother went silent when I went on about the West Coast.
Now, I startle easily at silent steps, something simple
someone needs—something to eat, something to keep
someone to stand side-by-side.

Aside, rib-to-rib.
A ribbing, to tease bonhomie.

I guess I had people on both sides of every gulf.
I guess my people eyed. Migrated. Mined.
Then I had a home on a dead-end. A park, popsicles, miniature golf.

Your own little history is a painted rock
you left by a taco truck, somewhere out there, those two weeks
last year.

There's a reckoning, I reckon
but I think you already knew that.

Shark Week Festival in Hellhole

We go looking for fun and find God Hates Unicorns. Red flag: hammerhead with a bloodlust laugh lurks left under the beer tent.[1] Meat truck sells rabbit-on-a-stick like my noodle-draping Nonna tried to teach me how to skin. After confiding "I am in love" she made a garlicky laugh "Little fish, you no lose pound."[2] Resurrected, the radio station of my roller-skating and rotary phone days broadcasts live. My gazelle-necked girl with yarn braids is tucked away in a heart-shaped WOMP-FM bait box. I take her out and you unpack your GI Joe fatigued little boy with a pop gun.[3] We throw them in like chum before unfolding our webbed aluminum chairs, daring fun to come and get us, to sink its rows and rows of antediluvian incisors into our moderately sagging, keloidal skin. "Get this," I say as you drink from a bedazzled horn, "the unicorn was a wild ass that sat in virgins' laps and something about salvation and hollow wombs."[4] You laugh like a schoolyard bully as you dig for singles to buy another drink. My chair collapses, my eyes roll back, I howl and as you wend through the crowd, I overhear some winged or finned creature breach: *Well, there is no fixing that.*

---

[1] 28% of Americans think the time to take up arms against the government is at hand.

[2] Did you mean Okie-Dokie? Noose? Rhinoceros? 46% of Americans mistake autocorrect for their subconscious.

[3] 83% of Americans think pop guns exemplify the successful deregulation of semi-automatic rifles.

[4] 326% of Americans believe pelicans are aerial fairies that collect aborted fetuses for cloud burials.

Memorial Day

Small blonde girl laughing
loose curls covering her ears

floating on a sea of buttercups
or discovering sand on a lip

of the Atlantic, it could have been
me. In the trenches, soldiers pinned

on her what they were fighting for.
America's armed forces aren't enticing

recruits—I read they're in the red
and they've circled back to

Be all you can be and some suggestion
or question about the provisions

in place should it be necessary
to reinstate the draft—I think I speak

narcissistically for an America wearing
its borderline personality disorder

on its sleeve when I say we love
those old black and whites

of our granddads in full dress
made to blush, blood rushing in

and out of them as they fought
for love of ... in silver frames on our

bookshelves whether we knew
their voices, the angle of their smiles

or their secrets second-hand, how
they carried us into picture windows

attached garages where they buried war
under standard-issue pistols and rifles

buried under hacksaws and dry-rot sneakers
under steps rising into a living room

where stars and stripes hung outside
the front door and potato salad was served

on picnic tables in the backyard where they
could cheer their sons rounding third.

One of mine, who's just a story, made it back
to a beer joint then onto boats until his heart

blew up on a barge before he could steer
clear of an estuary and another I knew well

into his ninth decade kept a sharp crease
in his khakis and every morning his corners

tight—to him I owe my subscription to National
Geographic this month featuring a fold-out

that maps one year of war in Ukraine. I am free
of notifications in hand regarding a cookout

or potluck or on my wrist where my pulse
is measured nonstop even at night when

my son plays Call of Duty and by day when
he puts up a good fight failing summer math

or loads mulch in truckbeds for guys he calls
old who smack his back, press five or ten

bucks in his palm and say something
that starts *Now, son, you listen to me ...*

Snowlessness

Winterly weather is predicted
but we usually escape storms.
I wait and pray to La Niña and post
my predictions to the eyewall.
Give us this day home from school
or work-from-home day.
It is cold and gray.
Pity me, blizzard, an overcast, haphazard human
and give me a weighted white blanket
silver powder for this dour
a need for fire
my life under glass
for an odd number of days.
Upwell my airy life
for a microburst, not by watch or warning
—advise me.
I am dry—meteorologically, astrologically,
cosmologically, and cosmetologically
and I am deeply buried
inside my skin. These long months
in between meaning
unfavorably prevail
and I beseech, yes beseech
(Ugh! These monotonous months
have me robbing frigid etymologies!)
you, Kevin at 7, not to mislead me.
I am as green as your screen.
Take my world and flake it, I am consumptively
clinging to the 7-day
arteries expanding with mercury.
I am adrift, weathering.
Mother, I need a whiteout timeout.
I need to be reminded
what keeps us safe and warm.

We paint the front door black after 20 years

Doors are such heavy metaphors
Studies show black increases saleability
so we've Cashed the ingress to our particular ring of fire

Knock-knock
Who's there?

All the old jokes are sitting around the donut shop
downtown sounding off about the good ole days
lacing up tricolor leatherettes, kicking down dupe doors
but the donut brunette rolls her eyes

Orange, she sighs

So you take door 2, you get the goat
we should talk more about inhumanism

I'm no door scholar, but I am a freak for peepholes

Maybe if I'd had more exposure to the old country
as a kid, but opening doors was for the rich
and I was poor

Maybe I need clowns and goats to cope
with deadbolts

Have you tried putting your ear in a glass, then the glass
to a door? Listen, if you don't want to eavesdrop
if you don't want to increase your saleability
if you don't want to come to some conclusion
about being human, puh-leeze

Perhaps it's time to reface your hell-for-leather face
Perhaps the time's arrived to open the mouth
that lets one eye in and keeps one out

What are we trying to prove with our gold
kickplate, our claptrap mat of what matters
our wreath of flowery vows

The time has come to lumber along like a woodchuck
in search of my shadow, like love lumbers along
unconditionally

To usher illusion in for a drink
Here's to the door of our doors, the passage of ways!

Come in, come in, to believe in beauty and mystery
to rediscover the tipsy forsythia, the ditzy deer, the unhinged
squirrels by the dozens, and the river, the old, old door
to all the crowd art our boneheads can hold

The bulk of us, that is, who are jammed behind doors
who measure the exact number of years, to the day
of events we call significant—our big days

Who spend a lot of time talking about
what's for dinner

False or not, we still want it all
to come through our spacetime gape, I guess

Occasional Poem

Your hand warmed the small of my back
after the sheets fell away

We made coffee and fire and checked out
of the world

Just as snow gathered, I found the mouth of a tunnel
hidden in you

and wandered along the secluded tiki-hut trail
yacht-rock path

How unexpected the little jungle, the soft, warm ground
the exotic rituals for laundry and lawncare

How unexpected bonobos drumming on hippos'
tummies

I mean, the full belly rhythm of you
is bonkers!

Birds playing musical chairs in prismatic
swallowtails and I swear

Tarzan barking *Swing yer partner* … as piratical dragonflies
mark the tangled liana

Ad libitum, I grab on to you grabbing on to a vine
and we do-si-do to-and-fro, waterfalling

I wasn't born in you, so we must be resurrecting
or relinquishing

Either way, I'm going to hangout on this side of the tunnel
in you today

I want to gather some heliconias and see how long
I can filter like a flamingo

Thank you, old-growth gods, for this blank day and everything
outside us overstrung

After all these years, to stumble into a newfound
tunnel, well, I will be

here watching monkeys comb through each other's hair
like the planet depends on it

As though each mite they pluck is the Gold Bond of bonding
the Gorilla Glue of commitment

After all, we are still teaching each other exactly what it is
we vowed to do

The Book Eaters

It all starts when someone says
My God the corn is so fresh
and everyone drawls butter
and then someone looks at me
over his steak knife and says
Read anything good lately
and with Jane Austen eyes
I toss a few titles (not Jane Austen)
into the cart like sweet peppers
and gold potatoes at Astromart
and then he sucks his lips
and tosses in a few jalapeños
and fresh garlic and before we know
what we're making, he's devouring
my titles and I'm devouring
his titles, neither of us is sleeping
he forgets he has kids
I forget my mother is dead
until we've devoured so much
it isn't enough—I have no choice
but to devour his spine
unbinding him, my pounding mouth
loosening every word of him
until each invertebrate syllable of him
is absorbed by plums or catfish
or onions or orioles or Orion
or scattered as light into a quasi-stellar
object not yet named—what choice then
have I but to uncover, to crack
my own vertebrae into exegetical discs
that wobble willy-nilly, weepy
and weeping, like a Jane Austen novel
for forgiveness until they sink
so far underground
they seed myth

4th Graders Answer the Question:
What Do You Know About Poetry?

Love
Stars and the moon
Words that rhyme
Like moon and harpoon
Like falling in love is like shooting
a harpoon through the moon
Or like the moon gets doom and gloom
when the harpoon misses
like losing your cereal-killer spoon
Like lucky stars shining
No, twinkling
No, flickering
No, winking
Like the moon is a whale
and the starlight piercing it a million times
is killing it but making everyone fall in love
No one knows what to do about love and death
so they cry
Sometimes you have to cry
especially when you are alone
in the dark
You can look at the stars
but no one really does look at the stars much
except scientists because it's their job
There are too many clouds and bugs and dishes and gas stations
but people still like to act like they look at stars
and talk about looking at stars
You can write about what you can't see
and stars are good for poems
or not good
Either way stars are actually dead
even though we think they're alive because it looks like
they're breathing
But they're so far away, we don't see them as they really are

so we can make them anything we want them to be
Like the story about the guy who chased a whale
or the story about the guy who got eaten by a whale
and lived inside it for a while and then lived
to tell the story about how he lived inside a whale
and dreamed about seeing stars again
though they're dead and he wanted to be alive
whether or not the whale was alive
How could they be alive together?
The moon is actually like a whale
the moon eats us alive and the stars
and we want to be alive, we want to eat and be eaten
as long as we're alive
Dark gets scary
So, mostly love

Orange

Grow heavy with sweetness
and hit the road, heavy
as Carmen Miranda's head.
I daresay my success metric
is making my own fruit hat.
I whip up ambrosia
because fluff is rarely
as frivolous as it seems.
An orange is never just
an orange alone. Proof:
orange oratory broke
my nose, poof!
Pulp and pith, I repeat
to remind myself, if it is alive
it means. Call me a pope
called to meaning, full
and less. Not to mention
a woman's head speaks
for her polysemy. I cobble
and preserve all fruits
sometimes spare and sour.
I don't mind bruises, but
rot I boycott because we
come from muck, pawpaws
dropped in Appalachia
or gushing oranges orphaned
in Valencia. Without fail, we come
from where we come from
too much or not enough.
Shady trees grow in every
grove. Teach me samba, tango
flamenco. Be warned, I'm
unconcentrated. I'm fashioning
a veil of pith for my face
to wear at the Orange Bowl

to sneak away for some creamy
mamey. Until then, I'll hold oranges
like a pitcher squeezing
for relief. I'll hold oranges
like a baby's head to feed.
Simple things bear our sweet
weight. For instance, an orange
disregarded makes whales
bellow on the beach. So hold it
against the mudflat, away
from the biting flies.
Tear the walls with care
and suck up the pulp
with fellow feeling because
this oeuvre is dense-in-itself
as are our brisk cravings.
Last words on any tongue,
they say, smell of orange.

CJ Farnsworth (she/her) is a poet residing in WV. She has a BA from Bethany College, an MS from Franciscan University, and an MFA from Vermont College of Fine Arts. Her poems have appeared in I-70 Review, Backbone Mountain Review, Appalachian Review, Kenning, Kestrel, Rattle, Women Speak, IMPOST, and others. She is a Pushcart Prize nominee.